Ano[...]
to fly

Anointed to fly

GLORIA WADE GAYLES

HARLEM RIVER PRESS
New York • London

Published for **HARLEM RIVER PRESS** by:
WRITERS AND READERS PUBLISHING, INC.
P.O.Box 461, Village Station,
New York, New York 10014

Copyright © 1991 by Gloria Wade-Gayles

Cover design: Janice Walker
Book design: Shey Wolvek-Pfister

This book is sold subject to the condition that it shall not, by way of trade or otherwise, be lent, re-sold, hired out, or otherwise circulated without the publisher's prior consent in any form of binding or cover other than that in which it is published and without a similar condition being imposed on the subsequent purchaser.

All rights reserved. No part of this publication may be reproduced, stored in a retrieval system, or transmitted, in any form or by any means, electronic, mechanical, photocopying, recording, or otherwise without the prior permission of the Publisher.

ISBN 0-86316-309-2 Paperback
ISBN 0-86316-304-1 Hardback
0 9 8 7 6 5 4 3 2 1

Manufactured in the United States of America

for

Mama!

who anointed me
and gave me her wings

for

Aunt Mae
who keeps them unfurled

The Poems

Part One
sometimes	3
Letters to Our Ancestors	4
Harvest	13
Rivers	14
Sometimes as Women Only	15
For My Lost Sisters	18
Talking for the Sisters	20
Women's Hands	21
Lava	23
For Those Who Are Trying to Understand Black Women	24
Untitled	26
A Woman's Lament	27
On Loving Me	28
On Falling in Love with Myself	29
On Celie	31

Part Two
The Concentrated Truth	35
Our Mothers' Silence	36
Trust	37
For Women Who Birth Daughters	39
Beatitudes for "Ladies"	41
A Foolish Question, Some Smart Answers	42
Initiation into Tenderness	46
A Mother's Gift	48

Celebrating My Children's Births	50
Successful Errors	52
Maternal Release	54
ChildrenMothers	55
For My Grandmother	57
Sunday Ritual	60
For Mama	62
Untitled	63
Acceptance	64
Grief	65

Part Three

Black Men	69
A Love Duet for Black Women and Black Men	71
A Primer for Black Women and Black Men	76
What Will You Remember, What Will You Forget?	79
Images	82
But Was It More than Sex Appeal?	84
Prince Albert Indeed: An Epitaph for My Uncle	87
A Mother Speaks about War	92

Part Four

Brogan–ed Life	97
For Revolutionaries	98

A Love Poem	100
Inquisition	101
Embrace	103
Heartwounds	104
Love's Name	106
Departure	107
Forgive Me	108
Loving Again	109
The Question	110
My People	111
Swords	113
Pessimism	115
Cracked	116
White Magic	118
On Hearing and Once Believing	120
"Come Back" to the Island	122
Nightmare	124
Rewind	127
??Glory Hallelujah??	128
The Pilgrimage	129
Beyond Gender	132
The Problem	134
A Black Woman's RSVP	135
Pretenders	138
To White Women Who Come with Words Only	139
For White Women Who Choose Liberation	142

And the Women Gathered	145
Feeling Low	154
Untitled	155
The Lesson	156
Platitudes	157
It's All the Same	158
Loss	159
Recovery	160
Unwanted Guest	161
When I Was a Child	162
Talking to Myself	164
For a Friend Who Considers Suicide	167
Fighting My Homophobia	169
Fear	172
Anointed to Fly	174

Part One

you wear your name well
sisterwoman of truth . . .

sometimes

    a
      woman's
        life
          is

              a
              fertile
              field

              sometimes depleted

              because no one
              rotated the crop.

Letters to Our Ancestors

To Sojourner Truth

you wear your name well
sisterwoman of truth

riding your chariot
hard and fast
through mud puddles
leaving brown tracks
on the faces of men
ashamed to show their arms

hard and fast
with your skirt raised
by your own hands
and your Bible raised
and your anger raised

hard and fast
through the births
and the thefts
and your mother's pain
which none but your Jesus knew,
and understood

you wear your name well
sisterwoman of truth
whose dressed-down words
rode hard and fast
through the centuries

arriving in time
and on time
to dressusup
for change.

To Phillis Wheatley

a million regrets we owe you
singer of songs
dancer with words denying
truth in every couplet
pain rhymed

they decorated you for royalty
we hanged you for treason

they stole your life
we threw away your art
which was the only life
you ever owned

a million regrets we owe you
sister poet
genius woman

mother of the free ones
writing freely

NOW

To Harriet Tubman

Time means nothing to those
whose suffering continues time
and time again to be ignored
by Time which takes no time
to end the seconds, minutes
hours and centuries of
our pain

It is time, I say,
to close the books
which lock you in a time
called yesterday
so removed from now that
only somebody else's words
can tell me who you were
and what you did
then

today
this moment

this second
(not a century ago)
but today
this moment
this second
I see your anger silencing a chorus of fears
your skirt brushing the earth clear of tracks
your courage calming the waters
your teeth
    biceps
       legs
          arms
               pulling the train to freedom.

To Ida Wells Barnett

from your womb
the children
you held with love
and released
for others to hold
while you held
the race

from your mind
the words pressed
into action
and history

from your rage
the knife
that cut the rope
and the gun
your woman's hands
would have cannoned
even at moving targets

To Mary McLeod Bethune

your dark skin and body
too large for dainties
meant by their definition
beauty was not yours

but it was not beauty you sought
or needed in their conference rooms

wearing the aroma of pies
passion
and the people's dreams,
you walked in
thunderously
sat down
proudly
took off your white gloves

ceremoniously
and moved your dark hands
fast
like scythes cutting through
thickets of lies

your lips
pursed with Africa
preached the plans
and sang the alma mater
yet to be

when you finished
talking and singing
         (you never danced for them)
you
left sane
with your bodacious hat
cocked arrogant
        and
              victorious

it was their world
their game
even their words

but your school

To Zora Neale Hurston

I want to resurrect you
the way you were
when you shook up
the patrons
and the writers
and the world
with your feisty genius
which didn't give a damn
about anything
except your truth

I want to remove
the pounds and the lies
and set you up somewhere
anywhere you want to be
with money
happiness
baaad hats
and a hundred Phoebes
holding your hand

To Fannie Lou Hamer

in Mississippi where
bosswhite men walked the earth

like gun-shaped shadows you
couldn't hide from
even in the dark

everybody knew
a Black woman didn't have a chance
to be free

in Mississippi where
the exact don't-miss-a-comma
recitation of the preamble, the
Constitution, the by-laws, and
Adam Smith's principles of dee-
mock-cracy were the hiddenbuttons
you had to push before the lever
would move,

everybody knew
an unschooled Black woman
couldn't go to Dee-See
and shatter the
chandaliers with her husky
you-gotta-listen voice for freedom

in Mississippi where
power wore white faces
and unzippered pants
or blonde hair teased
high like the hoods
they wore,

everybody knew a Black woman
owned by sharecroppers
didn't have a chance to
to become a business woman owning
so that the owning would stop

Everybody knew
a woman like you
had to sit down
stand back
give in
give up. . . .

you
refused
to
listen.

To All the Nameless Ones

you
opened
the
door
    and
      we
        have
          entered.

Harvest

If she claims her own planting ground;

If she selects her own seeds
and boldly, in the brightest of suns,
pushes them deep into the earth;

If she fights the weeds and worms
the bollweevils and bulldozers
with her own hands
and the frightful flying pests
with her own body,
formidable flesh,
not straw;

If she tills it and waters it
sings to it and dances for it
makes it fertile as she is fertile;

if she claims her own planting ground,

a woman's life is a harvest
bountiful enough for herself

and others.

───Rivers

Black women

   r
    e
     f
      u
       s
        e

to be

scenic ponds that have no depth,
majestic lakes that birthed no civilizations,
minor tributaries that run a course
other than their own.

We
are
rivers
wide
deep
insistent
powering

    R
    I
     V
      E
      R
       S.

Sometimes as Women Only

we know the hard heavy pull of weights
riveted to our dreams

and yet

sometimes as women only
do we gasp in narrow spaces
and remain locked behind walls
too rough for etchings from our soul

we are new queens of ebony
wearing diadems of natural beauty
feeling the swing of large gold hoops
around our tight-skinned smoothness

we walk a regal dance and sing
the music of a struggle
that names us well

and yet

as women only
we are sometimes marked beyond adornment
for we have seen white lines run
east west north south
cracking on our flesh like earthquakes
that no longer tremor
and we have felt the pressure of rigid staves
peaking breasts grown limp from the pull
of hungry mouths we alone can feed

we
are
fragile
figurines
whose neurosis, they say,
the moon creates
and controls.

and yet

we
are
monuments
that refuse to crumble and
deep-rooted oaks from which the generations
like thick-leaved branches grow
and thrive

we
are
the
strong
ones
having balanced the weight of the tribe
having made our planting as deep as any man's

and yet
as women
we have known only meager harvests

sometimes
as women only

do we weep

we whisper
when we wish to scream
assent
when we wish to defy
dance pretty on tiptoe
when we would raise circles of dust

before the charge

For My Lost Sisters

I have seen Black women wear
their resemblance to white beauty
like an over-sized brooch
on siliconed breasts.

They promenade seductively
away from the crowd
the better to be adored
the better to be photographed
for the cover of <u>Glamour</u>
and other magazines
that collect dust on salon tables.

I have seen educated Black women
tilt their heads in cocksure pedantry
and purse their lips to pronounce
profound words only radcliffe women
understand.

They wear their ivy-league degrees
and trips abroad
(to Europe of course)
like billboards that direct drivers
to exits out of the ghetto.

I have watched arrogant Black women
strut like peacocks in receptions,
tasting caviar, drinking champagne
and whispering like trained sophisticates
above the right music
(never jazz).

They wear their assumed importance
like gold plates on large paintings
in tacky nouveau riche homes.

I avoid brushing against their pedestals
'lest they topple
and
    f
      a
        l
          l
in paralyzing fear
to the world of Blackness
where all must drink
from a common cup of struggle.

For these lost sisters of mine
I say my ancestral prayers
and light ju-ju candles
to ward off the evil spirit
of self-anointed superiority.

Talking for the Sisters

(in case anybody cares to listen)

we don't want to gasp when we breathe
stumble when we walk
or squint, always squint,
because somebody removed the shade
and put the sun staring-close
in our lives

we don't want to read somebody else's
fine print in our contract or memorize
a history which skips over pyramids to get to
shackles because they can't deal with who
we have been and might once again become

we don't want to keep a ready supply
of flashlights and candles and matches
because somebody decided we look good
in the dark which is a contradiction
for people of the sun

we don't want to stay on our knees
moaning and groaning and praying
for miracles because whatever is wrong
somebody decided we can't fix it
by our selves, for our selves

We
just
want
to be
left alone

to
BE

Women's Hands

without a requiem
they buried us

a breathing mass of flesh and bones
of faces that were eyes that would
not close and bodies that were arms
and legs twisted and contorted
wrapped around thighs and necks and
breasts on top of breasts and ankles
locked to ankles locked in shackles . . .

but
    we
        continued
                to
                        breathe

and
    in
        the
            low
                places

we stood tall

an army of women
with hands
like shovels
like axes
like ploughs

working in silence

pushing through the solid wall of earth
hands tunneling to open places
and clapping like thunder
the miracle:

  WE
    SURVIVED

to travel throughout the universe
finding cracks
filling them in
covering them over
and planting in the new earth
flowers that will blossom
in all seasons

an army of women
with hands that say

no one else will be buried.

Lava

inside poor Black women
whose breasts have been stretched
to their knees by years of lactation
whose shoulders have been arched
by day work for white prima donnas
whose life has never been held
in another's hands
whose mirror has never promised beauty
whose face has forgotten the muscles
that make a smile . . .

inside these women
a volcano boils
preparing to erupt
and lava centuries of rage
onto a world that never understood
their pain

For Those Who Are Trying to Understand Black Women

You are searching for
trying to find
wanting to understand
Black women?

You want to look inside
our dreams and journey through
the dense forest of our desires?

You want to see us walk in bare feet
through alleyways of pain, stepping
on neglect and loneliness and your
prediction that we will bleed to death?

You want to hear us hum just hum because
we are sometimes too weary from singing
the blues to remember the words?

You want to see us in midnight lace
stroking our men whom
you have not found whom
you refuse to understand?

You want to touch our field-heavy
dishwater hands and trace the lines
that tell a story whose beginning
was the beginning?

You want to know how we do it
love
smile
dance
plan

achieve
dream
stay sane
and walk affirmed
in your world?

You want to know us,
Black women,
who do it all
in spite of it all?

First:

Do you believe in miracles?

Untitled

quietly
even with pride at the beginning
they carry the bricks,
one by one,
their wombs straining
as they build a castle
fit for a king
while the men they serve
in selfless love
count the bricks
yet to be laid.

A Woman's Lament

she is putting herself away
where faint glimmers of might-be
and exploding lights of must-do
cannot reach

her dreams are charcoals
in a furnace of frustrations
falling like cold cinders
into a life of
meals to be planned
stoves to be cleaned
dishes to be washed
children to be stroked
a husband to be understood

woman's work to be completed
and begun again
         and again

her song
a now-and-then note
in a harmony of lullabies
only women hum

her name
a half-spoken half-syllable
in a title of respectability
only women wear

her face
a catatonic smile of contentment
she dare not challenge

On Loving Me

(for my sister Faye)

Because I was weary of carrying
the weight of love,
I put my emotions on hold
and gave you my heart
for safe-keeping

"Keep it safe,"
I told you,
"from icebergs and heat waves
feasts and famines
vultures and tricksters
quacks and fanatics

"Hide it from petty women
who puncture hearts
with phony smiles
and from stunt men
who somersault hearts
and watch them fall
without nets
to the ground.

"Let the children feel its pulse,
but do not surrender it
even to them,
lest they break the strings
innocently."

In a box ribboned with love,
you returned my heart
undamaged
whole
healthy
and eight-chambered.

On Falling in Love With Myself

Too many people
have traveled to the inside
planted flags there
took one giant leap for themselves
and left me empty
locked outside
struggling to get inside
where the loving was,
where I took them,
even pulled them.

It was the woman in me
the mother in me
announcing to the world that
my breasts never run dry
my shoulders never sag
my legs can walk for centuries
and still run a marathon of giving

The varicose veins in my soul
speak the truth to me:
Even a strong woman becomes weary
from loving others
if she forgets herself.

And that is what I have done:
forgotten myself,
let myself go wanting
for pampering and prettying
stroking and resting.
I see that in my mirror
and in the eyes of friends
who wonder in what dark closet

I have hidden my beauty.

I am evicting all of them
even the good ones
who did not know they were using me up
and locking me out of my own soul.

I am going inside
to fall in love
with me.

On Celie

I have known many Celies

friends
neighbors
teachers
preachers
women from my past
women from my present
women with degrees
women of despair
prominent women who are envied
poor women who are avoided:

Black women in white America
walking with wounds
struggling with the heavy
weight of emptiness

I have seen them
like Celie
glance in cracked mirrors
quickly
sideways
at the Blackness
they believe explains everything
especially their pain.

Part Two

our
mothers . . .

The Concentrated Truth

our
mothers
pushed
us
out
of
darkness
into
darkness
and
became
our
light.

Our Mothers' Silence

In silence
our mothers watch us
fumble with our lives.

In silence
they watch
sophisticated scissors
cutting garments once worn by women
who at seventy
are stronger than we.

New women don't wear hand-me-downs,
we tell them.
We breathe deep,
rather than gasp.
We walk tall,
rather than stoop.
We shout jubilees of self
all over the land,
rather than sing sorrow songs
in dark and narrow rooms.

They could cure our disease of arrogance
and teach us about designs
handed down from generation to generation
for minor alterations,
and stronger threads.

But our mothers
watch in silence
and pray in silence
that we are not designing
patterns of confusion
for future generations.

Trust

at fifteen
my daughter took me gently
by the hand
and walked me
through the privacy
of her young life

she shared secrets
from a diary
kept in a not-so-hidden place,
reading them without comment
watching my face for
surprise
approval
or prior knowledge

she did not see my anger
when the neighbor's boy
tried to fondle her
or my pride when her
slim piano fingers
slapped his tight-skinned young face

she did not know
I had dusted her shoes with magic
that she would pirouette like
a real prima donna deserving
the thunderous applause my
hands made

she lingered with pride
on class election day
not knowing I had stuffed
the ballots with her name
and cut the stars into
confetti for her parade

she turned the pages fast
past her first love
whom I had burned in effigy
long before he broke her heart

she did not know
I needed no diary
to measure the width of her dreams
or the deep-cutting pain
of her disappointments

they had been mine
all mine
in silence

at fifteen
my daughter walked me
through the privacy of her young life

I do not believe
she will close the door
when she is older.

For Women Who Birth Daughters

the contractions will be
oceans rushing out of you
like a giant wave of pain

you will bear down
and bear them, pushing
her out packaged
tied to your center

the earth will tilt
when finally she ends her silence
and you begin your prayers
for her protection

because a girl child becomes a woman
       too soon

you will see the pinpoints in her chest
the open legs batting the air
and become at once a one-woman army
guarding the castle in which
you will cloister her

you will color her room with
flowers and harmless bears
dress her in ribbons bows
pearls white gloves

praying all the while that
the prescription for lady
will purify the air she breathes
and the minds of young boys

with high fevers and imprisoning hands

you will kidnap her
lock her in the closet of your fears
and walk into her dreams
carrying your own

but a wise woman
who has birthed a girl child
will show her all the open spaces
and release her to claim her own

after all
after birth
they cut the cord

Beatitudes for "Ladies"

"Heads up."
"Dresses down."

She wrote it on my birth certificate
printed it in gold in my Bible
and sang it as a refrain in all her lullabies.

Blessed are the shy girls,
she taught me,
for they shall be adored.

Blessed are the quiet girls,
for they shall be protected.

Blessed are the smart girls,
for they shall be admired.

Blessed are the pure girls,
for theirs is the kingdom of respectability.

Such was the catechism of my youth
and I was a devout convert.

I
have
been
shy
quiet
smart
pure

but
at forty

I am curious about the life
I have not lived.

I want to be a siren
and walk past a crowd of streetcorner men
my buttocks in painted pants
shaking desire to all who have eyes
my aroma a perhaps scent for
bloodhound men who leap at anything female.

I want to seal my sweet girl niceness
in a box no one can open.

I want to wipe away prissy kind smiles
cuss
bite
scream
burn to cinders anyone who tells me
not to how to when to what to.

I want to be a bad woman
who fights with a razor
sharp.

Even in heaven
(the place for all shy quiet smart pure girls)
I will be baad and mean and evil.
I will spend a night with Satan
collecting bawdy stories for angels
bored by the monotony of flapping
gossamer wings in pure air.

But for a woman
who has a daughter
beatitudes are lullabies
the after-birth did not remove.

She simply fantasizes about being
a baaad woman
and enjoys life in a
kingdom of respectability.

A Foolish Question, Some Smart Answers

My daughter broke from her cocoon
of shyness and out of curiosity
even desire
sat with her dancer's legs crossed
under a plain black skirt
before a panel of male judges
in search of a college queen.

She had expected kingly questions
that would place her as queen
at the center of the universe

but they asked her what **animal**
she'd like to be.

Her sweetness answered,
**"Deer
because
it is graceful gentle quick quiet."**

She is all of that
but I wish she had answered:

"owl"
        wise enough to see crooked bends
        hidden in the dark;

"giselle,"
        swift enough to reach rainbows
        before new storms wash them away;

"panther,"
>fierce enough to frighten away all
>predators and defeat those foolish
>enough to attack;

"eagle,"
>'gonna fly with my own strong wings
>as high as my dreams will take me."

I wish they had asked about
a **person** she'd like to be.

She would have answered
in her deer-like way

"Myself."

Initiation Into Tenderness

When my son sleeps with his first love,
I hope he will stroke her gently
and hold the full view of her in his eyes.

If she cries,
I hope he will kiss her tears
and confess that he, too, is like dew
that has fallen silently in a virgin forest—
fresh
gentle
untouched.

If she is uncertain,
I hope his arms will not imprison her
and his sweet words will not silence
the small voice that speaks of reason
in the presence of desire.

I hope he will free her
to meet his passion with her own
or, without explanation,
order the sunrise and leave him
unloved.

But
if
together,
they embrace the night,
I hope his lovewords will be
incantations the grateful
make to a generous god.

I hope he will love her tenderly
and promise to greet the day
with her
unashamed.

I hope he will love her as
no man will ever love her.

When they tire of their love
young grown old,
I hope he will speak her name softly
remember her gift with gratitude
and keep the sweetness of their nights
in the privacy of his memory.

A Mother's Gift

(for my children)

I want to give you a magic wand
because monsters stalk young and gentle
souls like you,
breathing fire and turning dreams
into charcoaled ashes.

But there is no magic in wands.

I want to give you music that never stops
because life can make screeching sounds
that test your sanity and tune out
the harmony of dawns breaking
unseen.

But nothing beautiful plays forever.

I want to give you understanding
clarity   strength   and direction
as direct as arrows that pierce the heart,
because you will need all of that
in the real world where you must
walk with padded feet
speak with tested truth
love with honest passion
where you must be whole
and ocean-deep in courage.

But I have emptied my coffers
and now in my winter years seek
like you
the filling places.

I want to make it right for you

well for you
happy for you
full and rainbow beautiful for you
even perfect for you.

But I can't take from you
the wondrous wonder of
walking through the forests
and finding your own clearing.

So
I'll just give you
my love
wings for your dreams
and my secret password
to the gods.

Celebrating My Children's Births

We remember
wanting you
needing you
asking the gentle winds
to search out the heavens
and find you—
because that's where you were
in the heavens

waiting to be called
so that you could
complete our lives
round us out
make us full
give us dawns

waiting to be called
by us,
the hungry dreamers.

And we called you
with passion
called you
with insistent
persistent
incessant
love sounds
called you
in private places
where we danced lengthwise
just for you
and no one could see
or hear

except the gods
who listened

planted you in our womb
grew you
delivered you

and birthed us
as one.

Successful Errors

I deserve no sceptre or throne,
no wings or shiny halos,
for mothers are neither queens nor angels.
Just ordinary people
who err and stumble.

I have done both.

I have chosen crooked paths
when straight ones directed me to truth.

I have made bouquets of fragile flowers
that withered expectedly overnight.

I have called the wrong names at the wrong times
and written notes to myself I never remembered to read.

I have been unsure
about everything
except your birth
except your name
except you,
my straight path.

My errors have been piercing splinters
too deep to be removed.

I have restrained you
restricted you
protected you

made demands on you
perhaps even dreamed for you.
I have used my imperfect hands
to mold a perfect life.

I
claim
my errors with pride
for they have kept you
from stumbling
and made you sure
of everything
especially
your paths
your flowers
your poems
and your dreams.
I know they have.
I know they have.

Look at you.
Just look at you,

wearing
wonderful
well.

Maternal Release

Last night
I cut out the tongue
that has wounded you
and threw it,
weighted down by errors,
into the deep oceans
my tears have made.

I shall not speak again,
except with my eyes,
and if they show anger
or disappointment,
I will sew them shut,
glue them shut,
close them
forever.

Last night
I removed myself
from your life
as judge
and jury
as dreammaker
and savior
because remaining
I anchored you
in needs
not your own.

I surrendered the life
I gave you at birth
and the nightmares began.

ChildrenMothers

Only yesterday
they sat locked
between the heavy thighs
of self-sacrificing women,
holding their heads still
as the women's loving hands
brushed their birth hair
into geometric designs
that had no blueprints
and like improvised jazz
could not be duplicated.

Only yesterday
they wrapped innocent legs
around the solid girths of fathers
who tossed them in mid-air cartwheels
like teddy bears that could not break
and carried them on broad shoulders
that were their thrones,
holding them steady even as
they were tickled where then
there were no breasts.

On yesterday
they were ghosts and goblins
pumpkins and pirates
sunbeams and elves
speaking trees
dancing raindrops
and Black angels
with coat-hanger halos
celebrating a virgin birth.

Today
we cannot hold them still between our legs
or touch them where now
there are breasts heavy with milk
and no one remembers or cares
that they were once young virgins
wrapped in homemade swaddling clothes.

Today
they carry the weight of lost innocence
and on city stoops
they sit alone
counting the months remaining
in an imprisonment that begins
when it ends.

For My Grandmother

I

She was born on dusty delta soil
her liquid round eyes at birth
reflecting dreams too deep
for dust-covered realities.

She was her own current
strong
directed
moving
the way she wanted
toward her dreams.

A proud woman,
she wore her Blackness
like a natural diadem.

A vain woman,
sure enough of her beauty
to strut high even on Dixie soil,
she strutted with defiance
from the cottonfields of her youth.

II

They tell me I am her child
darker and taller
without the marble eyes
and the cold black hair
without the exploding rage
that kicked Mississippi dust

into white faces
without the beauty
that made mirrors break into song.

But
Her
Child.

And that is why.
they tell me,
I never cared for fairy tales
about kisses that turned green frogs into
prince charmings and never thought
little boy blue and his trumphet had
anything to do with my life.
She taught me to make my own music
to find my own heroes
to turn myself into a princess
by myself.

III

There should have been more
than the slim eulogy
brief songs
and fragrant flowers forced into designs.

The white-gloved men
mere mortals
with strong backs and long arms
closed her from me

pushed the painted box
too fast   too fast
into an open earth.

There should have been more.

In death's satin silence
she spoke to me,
her voice gently shaking
autumn leaves into my hair
designing a crown
for me
her child.

And I could feel myself
becoming her current
continuing strong
      persistent
      defiant

Sunday Ritual

homemade biscuits
fried-crisp bacon
cheap margarine puddled
in a mound of grits

two kisses
sometimes three
a hug
a smile
a dime for the collection plate . . .

and Mama stayed home.

She had no use
for church folk
church hats
church gloves
and church paint
spread thick on faces
that gulped down
churchy words.

I concealed my shame in
my Sunday-go-to-meeting smiles
and above the sounds of
the tinny-voiced choir
I prayed in silence for her salvation.

Today
at sixty
she testifies for blessed assurance
sings of gossamer wings
all god's chariot-watching children wear

smiles religious under a halo of gray,

and prays for my salvation.

I have no use now
for empty rituals
and churchy things
long ago mildewed,
born in the beginning
of an insidious word.

I sing of a new religion
created in the empty spaces
the old one never filled.

I raise a revolutionary chant
of Blackfaith based on Blacklogic
that will do more for Blackpeople
than the sugarpill hymns
Mama sings.

She hears me out with a smile
closes her eyes
and singing of amazing grace
she tells me about her god
who is real
and listening
wayupthere

where
no one can prove
he is not.

For Mama

It's always out there,"
you said,
"trying to get inside
where it belongs."

You cleared a path for it

opened shutters
      windows
      blinds
      drapes
pulled the door off its hinges
and stripped away top branches
    from tall tress

You traveled to the sun
touched its center
and with singed hands
you brought back the light
and put it into my heart,

"where it belongs,"
you said

you had prepared me
to meet darkness
illuminated within.

Untitled

It has come to this
your eyes tell me
      aging
      regret
      loneliness
      and memories your forgetfulness
      will not let you forget

You have propped yourself
in a rocking chair
moving nowhere waiting
to hear them call your name

I will not let you fix your failing eyes
on white-robed angels beckoning
you to a faraway in the sky world
where there is no need for mothers
because there are no tears

I want you to laugh again
and braid sunlight into your hair
I want you to claim your life
because it does not yet belong to heaven.

I have muted Gabriel's horn
and locked the pearly gates.

I will not let you leave me,
my flanneled queen,
not now
not ever.

Acceptance

I feared my mortality
the eternal silence
that will force those
who love me to search
their memory for
my throaty voice
my off-key songs
and the laughter
I now muffle with
hands never manicured.

I had nightmares
about the darkness
and the distance
and the dampness
I know will be unbearable
because I will have to bear them
alone.

I feared feared my mortality
until I saw you accept your own
with dignity
and a knowing smile.

Grief

My friends tell me I have lost my mind
that nothing moves or speaks
or hears in this place
except nameless men in faded blue
who open and then close the earth
dispassionately.

I tell them,
"It is not my mind I have lost,"
but those who have not seen
the cutting of the cord that gave them life
cannot understand.

Cannot.

When gentle birds dance their ownership of the sky
or cloister themselves in secret places from a storm,
at dawn or at dusk,
I drive in silence,
knowing the road without seeing it,
past numbered sections of earth
where alabaster women men and children
with unchanged expressions
look to the heavens
that did not answer.

I drive on
without the cortege of mourners
who could not mourn
past open spaces yet unfilled

past green tents staked to the earth
past flowers stapled to wire
ribboned
addressed
and left to turn to dust above the earth.

There were no fences around your life
but here there are fences
and a large gate too fancy
for the simplicity of a life
that locked out no one.

I reach your number
and steady of step now,
I walk toward the huge oak tree
that won my heart on selection day
to
your
name
now in bronze.
I talk to you.
I talk to you
because
because

even in this fenced-in world of silence
I want you to hear my love.

Part Three

Black Men
are . . .

Black Men

Black Men
are

Stallions

kicking
bucking
biting

Stallions

refusing their backs
to those who come
with maps
ropes
saddles
and
spurs
sharpened

They gallop
gallop
gallop away
fast fast fast fast

like wild Stallions

making winds of dust
leaving no hoofprints
galloping fast
to open fields of their dreams

where no one can break them in
tame them
train them
name the trails for them.

Black Men
are also
high-stepping
footprinting
dancing gentle

Stallions

who cushion their backs
for those
without spurs
who ride light
with stroking hands.

A Love Duet for Black Women and Black Men

Listen, my brother.
Listen.
I love you.

You must know
I love you.

The hand that reached beneath the shackles
to feel your pulse
was my hand
The voice that disturbed the waters
we rode together
like cargo we rode the waters
was my voice
The body that bore your children
and theirs
was my body
The prayer that called your name
was mine
The dream that kept you alive
was mine

I love you.

You are my sun,
my African sun,
sitting atop Kilimanjaro.

I lift my eyes to your beauty.

I love you.

Listen, my sister.
Listen.
I love you.

You must know
I love you.

The hands that spreared those
who stole you from Eden
were my hands.
The voice that rumbled like thunder
through the holes of slave ships
was my voice.
The body that bore the lash was mine
The prayers
the dreams
the heart overflowing
flowing over with pain
our pain

all were mine.

I love you.

You are my moon,
my African moon,
dancing at midnight
on the bosom of the Nile
wherein I am baptized.

I love you.

My brother,
I have lain with you in lands
which love owned
which pride named
where peace traveled
like a sweet stream
that had no beginning and no end

I love you.

My sister,
I have danced with you in lands
where meadows knew no boundaries
and valleys were our lovebeds
stretching soft beneath mountains
which if they could have spoken
would have echoed our names.

I love you.

You are my African moon.

And you are my African sun.

We are together our own heaven
and our children are the stars

They who would divide us
know nothing of this love
born at the beginning

this love born in the beginning
with us, the beginning.

On the canvas of my mind
they paint a picture of you
I do not recognize.

And they stretch my woman's lips
with strange names for you
I cannot speak.

They are designing our destruction
by denying our love.

They are walking into our lives
carrying chaos.

We open the door for them.

We seat them like royalty.

And the loving stops.

And the pain begins.

Only our love
can keep them out.

We are our reason
for struggling
for dreaming
for being
man
and woman:
        only the gods can change that.

Listen, my sister.
I love you.
I will show the world
how much I love you.

Listen, my brother.
I love you.
I will show the world
how much I love you.

You are my African moon.
I love you.

You are my African sun.
I love you.

Listen.
I love you.

Listen.
I love you.

A Primer for Black Women and Black Men

the simple
elementary
truth: only we together
can save the people.

the profound
fundamental
indisputable
truth: only we together
can save the people.

We
Together
      can kidnap those can do
but won't do for the people
kidnap them, blindfold them,
lay them in the back seat of
deluxe models, and race
them home

We
Together
      can walk the alleyways and
the avenues
sit in the pews and the
parlors
work in the fields and the
kitchens
teach preach love and sing
on key
the nation-song.

We
Together

>	can convince the West Wind
>	and the East Wind
>	the North and South winds
>	to push the debris
>	in our lives to the edge of
>	the world and with
>	our breath we can blow it
>	over.

We
Together

Working
Together

>	can change the world
>	for our people

The simple
elementary
truth:
>	Only we
>	Black women and Black
>	men can save the people.

The profound
fundamental
indisputable
truth: Only we
           Black men and Black women
           can save the people

           and ourselves.

I mean I mean I mean . . .

Just what kinda rock would
Gibraltar be

divided?

What Will You Remember, What Will You Forget?

yes
believe them

we have prepared a woman's room
our own space
an oasis for our souls
where we are alone
with songs remembered
from the nakedness of birth
which we are singing in our own key.

but do not
believe them
when they spit out untruths
about mountains   moats   mines
and man-eating monsters trained
to find the juggulars of our men.

yes
believe them

this is our room scented
with our breath steamed
with our passion for talking
walking   dreaming   testifying
be-
ing
affirmed whole
women

but do not
believe them

when they say we have banished you
from the kingdom of our desires
because our creation was meant
all along to be your destruction.

you must remember
treason was never ours
not in the beginning
and not now

we rode the waters with you
and as if our love could remove
the shackles
we loved you
we called your name and ours
our name and yours
oursyoursouryours
one name
in one piercing scream for freedom

yes
believe them

we dance a mean
liberation rhythm

but do not
believe them
when they say
hating you was in our plans
to love ourselves.

if you forget to remember
that we have been with you
through everything

you will believe them

and fly like Black moths
to a flame of division
those in power
will never willingly
extinguish.

Images

I am weary of the truths
about some Black men
woven into masterpieces
and presented as gifts
to those who do not understand
the truths are half-truths
made by their untruths.

I am weary of the "picture show"
that flashes in color
stereo
with special effects
on a screen large enough
for a long parade of us
digging graves
but reciting no eulogies
because the dead are our men
without names
without worth
without eyes that can see
promised horizons.

I am weary of the pain
of seeing our pain a performance
applauded in chandaliered halls where
made-up made-over made-false
women in sequins satins
woven hair and tinted eyes
hold a gilded cup with grateful hands
because they played our destruction well.

I am weary of gagging on it all
and screaming epithets at those

who have forgotten the danger
of moving half-truths like
pendulums for national hynopsis

I weep
close the books
turn off the screen
walk outside . . . .

I weep again.

Harder.

But Was It More than Sex Appeal:

Remembering My Father

Mama says
sex appeal does not come in a size 42 suit
or in hair that lies slicked down
fluffy or curly at your command.

It doesn't come in a bottle either,
she says,
"cause if it did
everyone with cash could buy it
retail
and if they are greedy
wholesale."

It doesn't speak
pretty sweet words through
pretty teeth straight enough
to be pillars for a temple

and it doesn't always perform
you know, perform,
when no one is looking or knowing
or feeling except the lovers.

"It just **IS**,"
she says,

and adds,
"Your father had it."

I see you in brown pictures
too torn for cardboard corners
that mount our lives—

the gap that disturbs your smile
the nose spreading above broad lips
that spoke home-style rhyme.

You are smiling
in Mississippi work pants
in cheap Chicago street suits
in a gray baseball uniform
from the days when you thought
Jackie Robinson was lucky
because you weren't
and broadest when you stand
in the small Calumet parlor
with a trumpet in your right hand
a white handkerchief in your left
because you knew how to do it
before Satchmo,
and better.

There are no pictures of the other women
who loved you,
but I can see them fussing over you
seductively straightening your wide ties
and putting up the Stetson you wore,
they said,
at a sexy angle.

I flip through the mental calendars
they made of your face
for every month of the year
and read your words that were
their quotes to live by,

to plan nights for.

I ask Mama
why all the women loved you
would have followed you to hell
had that been your destination.

She only answers,
"Your father had it."

I understand why you dared
speak your own name in a world
that denied you everything
except what they feared
you had
      naturally.

But it wasn't sex appeal
that kept you sane in this world
dancing-singing-dreaming sane.

It was Mama
loving you
loving all of you
always loving
all of you

Mama holding you
just holding you
quietly
gently
holding you with tenderness
holding you without interest
in your sex appeal.

Prince Albert Indeed: An Epitaph for My Uncle

An odd name they gave you,
my uncle,
Black hoboman
Black streetwalking man
Black PRINCE Albert indeed
who never knew robes.

They called you Beale Street Red
the Black man with hair the color of sand
shaking the cards
pulling magic from your slim fingers
and singing naughty songs for people
who drank down their laughter
and forgot to dream.

You were the poet of the lost ones
most brilliant
when sweet wine made your rhythms quick
and your rhyme long syllables of
wind-blown desires.

I loved you,
my uncle,
even when you shamed me
I loved you.

I loved you as a child loves
a game
a diversion
a clown wiser than paying spectators
a somersault going higher
turning nowhere.

I loved you acting out poems
you had penned from your soul
or making poems that rhymed
with the aroma of cheap wine
and then being a poem sad
you recited with bitter laughter.

You made your life a game
shattering rules written for those
who must always lose,
even the small stakes,
you said.

And you
won your lost life
well.

We dressed you in brown,
they placed you in bronze
sleeping without breath.

At last you were your name
A Prince whose long poem had ended.

In the stillness there was rhythm
and I could see your smile
like a crooked river finding its source
In the silence there was rhyme
and I could hear your laughter
making new poems
and polishing the old ones

that had named you

>   Beale Street Red
>   Funny Man
>   Game-Playing Man
>   PoetMan
>   My Uncle
>   Prince Albert.

For Our Sons

Our sons are dying
        but there are no graveside ceremonies
        of smooth–valved taps
        and white–gloved salutes,
        no flags folded in mid–air
        by brass men walking
        stiff–legged in reverence.

Three blocks from the backyard petunias
they once pulled
Our sons are dying

A stone's throw from the church
where they sang, "Yes, Jesus loves me,"
Our sons are dying

Outside the gates of football fields
where their biceps "held the line,"
Our sons are dying

In places that wear the colors
of their youth
Our sons are dying

carrying light artillery
that explodes in their veins.

Those whose pockets are heavy with power
come to us with clinical concern
and in language cold enough to freeze the heart
they speak of percentages
and then of causes
which condemn us

even as they shroud us in grief.

Percentages do not
breathe
or dream
or die
and those with power
are never without blame.

We know the truth:
Our sons are dying
in an undeclared war
which profits those
who do not know
or love
our sons.

And so a call to arms
to people who have known wars
and won even those they lost:

For every son slain,
we shall save ten thousand.

For every son slain,
we shall save ten thousand.

For every son slain,
we shall save ten thousand.

A Mother Speaks About War

Once is enough.

That's what my eyes told them
when they came to my door

with fervor and flags
redwhiteandblue pretty
and yellow ribbons
only those who have lost
no roots can use

symbols of patriotism
brand new for the new war
storming in the sand.

"Support the war,"
they said,
"to support our troops."

"It's about remembering when
the men came marching home
to deserted streets and a
defeated nation biting its lips
in shame.

"Support the war,"
they said again,
"to support our troops."

Above the sound
of "bombs bursting in the air,"
they who have lost nothing
who have no emptiness where

once there was a beating heart
could not hear the mournful sound
of taps even the spirituals
cannot drown.

Theirs is a mosaic of patriotic pictures
spit-shining boots
and parades for heroes
silenced forever in distant lands.

I wanted to tell them,
the issue is not
the issues of war,
right or wrong,
but war itself

Only with my eyes
did I tell them,

I gave,
and the last war
took away.

Once is enough.
Once should be enough
for
all
of
us.

Part Four

Tiptoeing is fine
when you are walking . . .

Brogan-ed Life

Tiptoeing is fine
when you are walking
through fields of clover
or in a moist cool valley
the pioneers did not find.

You can take off your shoes
and walk gently
certain that only soft grass
and damp soil will cling
to your feet
and nature's blossoms will cushion
your head in a fall.

But we do not walk in fields of clover
and the pioneers left no valley undisturbed.
There is no cushion for our

                f
                 a
                  l
                   l
                    s.

So I say
NO
to tiptoeing.
I want to walk hard
and firm.
I want to wear thick-soled brogans
laced up to my thighs,
a hard hat,
a suit of metal armor
and something
something
to protect my heart.

For Revolutionaries

"Revolutionaries
don't write love poems,"
they tell me
with clenched teeth,
their fists raised
beyond my touch.

Revolutionaries
write martial words
warriors chant before the charge.

"We have no time for love,"
they say,
looking at the moon
through the barrel of a gun
and feeling good
when the trigger does not jam.

"Love softens us,"
they tell me,
"sweats our hands
takes our breath away,
and makes us forget
war is about dying,
not love."

They tell me again,
emphatically,
in case something in their voice
did not ring true:
"Revolutionaries do not write love poems."

I sharpen their blades

grease their cannons
fix their bayonets
lace their boots
snap on their helmets
and in the flickering lights
of battles distant
and yet so close
spent shells shatter my peace,
I sit down to write

love poems
which sing of sweet nights
when revolutionaries
naked of guns
surrender with pleasure
to the only passion
that makes sense of it all.

A Love Poem

(for Joe)

a casual pat on my backside
the throat-low tone of your hello. . . .
tonight we will light tall candles
and dance lengthwise to their waving motion
in the darkness of our room.

I rush the children through
the ritual of bedtime stories
and hand-clasped prayers
and when like cherubs
they curl up for dreams,
I prepare for the night.

When the candles burn low
into sculptured designs,
I purr to the rhythm of your gentle strokes
and my body becomes a breathing, sighing
singing ribbon wrapping the gift
that bears only my name.

When we are four times twenty,
and passion has become a naughty smile
on faces with dressed up teeth,
we will move from our rocking chairs
to a love bed age has made softer
burn taller candles
and end the night in the after-joy
of love.

Inquisition

Do you love her?

Yes.

Do you begin your prayers with her name?

Yes.

Have you trained the nightingales to sing her favorite song, continuously?

Yes.

Have you carved her face on Gibraltar?

Yes.

Have you built a boardwalk over the oceans and the seas so that she can walk on water?

Yes.

Have you traveled through the desert in search of a velvet cactus just for her?

Yes.

Have you substituted your dreams for her nightmares?

Yes.

Do you speak her name in a gentle whisper

and only with her permission?

Yes.

Do you stroke her back
massage her feet
fluff her pillows
draw her bath
cook her meals
brush her hair
dress her in
         silks and satins
         sables and minks
         pearls diamonds
         rubies ermines
         and glass slippers
         that cannot break?

Yes.

Do you love her?

Yes!
Yes!
Yes!

Is
She
White?

SILENCE.

Embrace

Some men's hearts are like granite
        cold

        un
        yielding

        im
        penetrable

But yours,
my love,
is like the fertile earth
after a spring shower

                soft

                warm

                moist

                wrapping itself
                around the roots
                of my being

                and I become
                a flower
                thick-blossomed
                layered in beauty

                a perennial
                love made.

Heartwounds

Some men have not learned that heartwounds
as deep as a woman's need for love
do not respond to phoney curatives
of roses, sweetened words and
make-up passion in scented rooms.

They do not heal themselves
with the passing of time
which erases time only
but not pain and the memory
of pain.

Left untreated
heartwounds become
sores
scabs
scars
ugly reminders of flawed love.

Some men believe
women were born
to endure
to understand
to forgive
to be irrational in all things.

It is that way,
they tell us,
with the pull of the moon.

They will not learn
perhaps cannot learn
that a woman's heart

damaged by multiple wounds
beats faintly

and then

not
at
all.

Love's Name

Mine was an uneventful life
then
a flat movie of flat scenes
I walked into but did not write
and could not play forever.

Slick squares of cellophane
turned on iron hard reels
and images clicked fast
through a channel of light
catching dust particles in mid-air

and there I was
a role projected on a white screen
singing songs Beale Street never set to music
stretching my lips for canned lines
that never called my name

We
burned the cellophane
turned on Beale Street/Birminigham sounds
put up a new screen
and projected images
of you
and me
standing centerstage
in our love.

Departure

(for a friend who chose to leave)

Without tears or requests,
she departed.

She could have written a goodbye,
explaining how weary
she was of eternal winters,
but she was out of words,
written or spoken,
having wasted them in her
pleas for spring.

She could have walked wounded
into a penthouse suite
and recounted the saga of her empty life
for a horn-rimmed lawyer
trained to find the juggular,

but she wanted nothing
to weigh her down
trip her up
turn her face to his
which would give half answers
to questions she no longer
cared to ask.

Besides,
there was nothing he could give her now
except her wings stored
in a locked closet
only he
for years
could open.

Forgive Me

Forgive me
if I forget to say
"Forgive me"
when I forget to love you
with my words
my hands
and especially
my eyes.

Loving Again

Last night
we loved as if the gods
had announced only to us
that the sky would fall
while we slept.

We loved
passionately
selflessly
thinking only of pleasure
giving pleasure,

and I knew I would not grieve
if life should end as you held me.

Daybreak.

The sun slid silently
into our room
kissed our faces
and lay softly
in our love bed.

The sky had not fallen.

The earth had not disappeared.

We were alive
to love again.

The Question

Is it proof of our martydom
or a sign of our insanity
that we have walked into burning forests
and emerged,
flesh hanging from our bones
with smiles and songs
and sermons about hope?

My People

My People Sleeping
comatose in the wasteland
hooked up to machines with frayed wires
Wake Me.

My People Playing
white with their hands,
their eyes, their speech,
their choices (like white anything
is better than Black everything)
Pain Me.

My People Running
fast and scared
from our birthplaces
never looking back or
remembering or caring to remember
Anger Me.

My People Exploiting
my people or any people
because somebody's sacrifices
gave them degrees and checkbooks
which they want to make fatter
and fatter at any human cost
Disgust Me.

My People Loving
my people
struggling for
my people
changing the world
for my people
for all people
Make Me Proud to Say

"**My People.**"

Swords

They wrote no wills.

They left no estates.

In chains they could
bequeath no heirlooms.

But they left us their swords,
passed them on to us
sharp swords
that know how to swing
heavysharp swords that
can fell walls and systems
that will not fall
unless with swords
you tear them
      d
        o
           w
              n.

In our world,
a fake clearing
for the chosen ones
whose names the mad magicians
pull like rabbits' ears
from trick hats turned
upside down,

the swords are too dull

to crease the tongue
of those who have chosen
not to speak of swords

But the children's tears
are like acid
removing the rust
restoring the swords
making their edges
as sharp as the children's pain.

We must hold them
in our steady hands
and

  s
   w
    i
      n
        g

them

until . . . .

Pessimism

sometimes I feel
Blacklife is

halftime
an offbeat time
timed counter
to harvests
an offbeat halftime
away from OURtime time
an offbeat halftime
spent fast on hours
dragged slow on minutes
clustered around seconds
gathered into confusion
and diaphonous gains

Sometimes I feel
Blacklife is
a faceless clock
set at zero
sounding a constant alarm
no one can shut off.

Cracked

seven years ago
or more
we heated it in the intensity of our dreams
making it strong and shatterproof
that it would endure
tremors and quakes
and explosions
        carefully planned.

with tears from eyes
that had seen the vision
we polished it
shined it
cleared it of streaks
and blurs and distortions
        carefully designed.

in jubilation
we dressed for it
scrubbed our skin
clean of paints and creams
that run when tears fall
and circles of red that become
displaced when tight-skinned faces
wrinkle for thick-lipped smiles

we grew Afros for it
tilling them well
until each strand
was a natural harp playing

the melody of true reflections

in seven years
or more
we lost it all

in perms and pomades
in mass produced eyes
the colors of the rainbow

in Black men
sleeping away the day
under steel bonnets

in Black children cuddling
Barbie Dolls blonde
dressed in Fifth Avenue originals

for seven years
or more
no one asked questions about our beauty
for we were clear reflections of the answer.

the mirror is cracked

we will wander
through seven years
of harsh distortions.

White Magic

perhaps it was
the scorching
soul-burning
low-down
never-setting sun
under which we

tilled the soil
harvested the crops
laid the railroads
built the bridges
and sang the songs
that colored us happy
in
their
book.

perhaps it was
the daytime
nite-time
anytime
screams of women
struggling against erections
of power and lust
or the midnight growls
of bloodhounds scenting
men who would be returned
alive to lean helplessly
into circles of death

it might have been
the catechism of short sentences

and lying words
about a white god who decreed
that we should be dark worshippers
worshipping in the dark
riding imaginary chariots
to an imaginary heaven
we could enter
only if we endured
          the signs
          and sheriffs
          and shotguns
          and prodders
          and police
          and mobs
          and dogs
          and hoses
          and chains
          and . . .

but I believe
it was white magic
imported to this god-forsaken place
to cauterize our brain.

Why else
do we still fight in the quarters
while they watch entertained
from the veranda of the big house?

On Hearing and Once Believing

i heard them

lawd knows i heard them
down south
way down deep
into cotton

i heard them
when i was young
anxious
delicate
when i couldn't dream
for hearing them

the long loud dixie yell
of ya'll folks lies
the american anthem sounds
of anthologized
spiritualized
ritualized
myth-lies
screeching and screaming everywhere
even in the church of the blue-eyed god
and in the fake hymns
that almost drowned the spirituals
that heard them,
then mourned.
deep down there
where hell was
a southern crop
growing in barren soil,

i heard them
and lawd knows

we
believed
them

THEN.

"Come Back" to the Island

The white commercial
invites us

"Come back"

to the island
the sun-kissed white beach
of umbrellas
Oil-of-Olay
Ralph Lauren shades
Waldorf Astoria towels
Gucci wraps
and other props for fun
the rich and restless leave behind.

"Come back"
to the island
to waters clearer
than the crystal
from which they drink the best year
and bluer than their eyes

"Come back"
to the island
to full moon nights
and sensuous men
tanned without the sun
who dance the phallic limbo
and lay us down on microscopic
grains of sand that make
no love sounds.

Black people

go back
to the island

and see
the blue sky
the full moon
the white sand
clear waters

and our people

serving elegant pleasure
to others.

Nightmare

they remove me from my four-poster bed
and place me blindfolded
naked
in the sandbox
i had known
as a child

clearly
i see the hundred
carbon copy redbrick units
of my old life
and the sloping hill
i wore thin of grass

i hear the voices of women
whose small collard patches
i destroyed on halloween
whose red and pink roses
i picked on mother's day
whose errands i ran
when pads were worn
whose daughters i fought
whose sons i loved
whose dreams once named me
"Sunshine."

i am ashamed
of my new life of

carpets and chandaliers
champagne and caviar
maids and Mercedes
diplomas and degrees

private lawns
private schools
pretty words
pretty people
the pretty life
they have not known

the small box widens
and i am in a tunnel
whose exits are sealed
and i become a child
running from eyes
that scream silently
"Have you forgotten?
Have you forgotten?

i awake
in a dry stinging sweat
i awake
knowing that i have wrestled with truth
or worse with the souls of women
who expect small returns
from giving that heaves
in large bosoms

tomorrow
i will journey from my world
of pampered lawns
pampered cars

and pampered people

to the unpampered women of my youth
to explain why and how and when . . .

night comes
and i hold back the sleep
until morning is a rose dot
carried on the wings of birds
who refuse to sing

i reach for my potient
of valium and dry wine

again
it is mixed with sand.

Rewind

The young ones are beating drums
taut with rage and dancing
judgment on the revolution
which wasn't.

There were no warriors there,
they tell us,
only patients fighting the knife
succumbing to the ether which
made you go light-headed
through the motion of going
through the motion of
revolution.

They
will
teach
us
how it should have been done
back when we thought we did it
so that they wouldn't need to do it
again.

"A real revolution."

We listen
take our blows
rewind the tape

and smile.

??Glory Hallelujah??

Holding deluxe Bibles
with manicured hands
pale faces sit self-righteous
in the crystal church
wiping away missionary tears
as the regal Indian
denies his gods
and sings to Jesus

forgets the reservations
and hits high notes
for America

The Pilgrimage

Two decades had passed
when I began the pilgrimage
dressed in dungarees
and pride
walking to the rhythm of memories.

I sang Movement songs along the way
holding a picket sign
    FREEDOM
in my left hand
and a tight fist
    BLACK POWER
in my right.

Drivers in long sleek cars
honked their horn.
I raised my right hand
and smiled.
When they stopped
where there were no red lights,
I held the picket sign
like a printed card
for a 20-20 vision test.

Passersby in three-piece suits
walked close enough to touch
our tears and to smell the odor
of human bodies crowded into
makeshift southern jails

I greeted them with
our old hello:

POWER TO THE PEOPLE.

To adults who should have remembered
I was a preacher proselytizing
for a dead religion or a street woman
without bags announcing to the world
"I have lost my mind."

But to the children who followed me
out of curiosity
wonder
and strange reverence,
I was a prophet bringing a message
they understood
but could not name.

I marched on,
calling the places by name

Selma
Montgomery
Anniston
Atlanta
Philadelpha
      (Mississippi)
Jackson
Orangeburg . . . .

Even when heavy rains
made FREEDOM a smudged design
I marched on

I had expected a well-painted sign

    HERE THEY ONCE WORKED
    TO CHANGE THE SOUTH.

or something that proved
it was real
we were real
the pain was real
the deaths were real
and had meaning.

It was our shrine
abandoned
in a wasteland
of glass and bricks
and bent cans
and cars without tires
and houses without doors
and men without hope.

On the porch where once
we had hugged our dreams
and each other

a gaunt Black woman
rocked in loneliness
and looked past me
with cataracted eyes.

Beyond Gender

It could not have been otherwise,
they say,
because the world has been ruled
by men with hands
too rough to feel the human pulse.

If women had been in charge,
they say,
history would have been a sonnet,
its rhyme honey sweet
its images rich
in the colors of spring.

I am not convinced
by what they say.

Women
wrapped willing legs
around the loins of men who
captained slave ships
stoked ovens
fixed bayonets
aimed cannons
pulled triggers
tightened ropes
dropped bombs
and in thick-volumed books
justified their world.

Nothing has changed.

Today
women

starch the shirts of men
who molest child
prepare feasts for men
who batter wives
and sit reverent in Sunday worship
with men who have mastered
the art of lying
even to God.

In designer clothes
that have no duplicates,
they sit in high places
like smiling mannequins
hostessing affairs of state
where men play Russian Roulette
with our survival.

Women have been trained
as silent spectators
or willing accessories
to the folly of it all,

and sometimes
with manicured hands
women alone have designed
devious plans for human suffering.

If women had been in charge,
it would not have been otherwise,
for women are not born into sainthood
and goodness, like evil,
has no sex.

The Problem

the problem was
we expected too much
we were too eager for a settlement
to read the fine print

on assignment
which we did not know
was
assign-ment
we returned with legal pads
to the neighborhoods of our youth

for data
to fill the empty columns
marked for us
to be analyzed by them

the problem was
we expected too much
we believed it
would seed a new world
for women
all women

that this was the real thing
a **woman's** movement
whose kaleidoscopic concerns
would make Black
a dominant color

the problem was
the old problem:
we expected too much

A Black Woman's RSVP

You must understand my reasons
or can you?

You see
I thought they were proud
of the papers and the speeches
I gave at conferences they didn't call.

I thought they were bragging about
their dark child integrating panels
being "the expert" who knew it all
and said it well in language
they never spoke.

UNTIL
Miss Rosie from my old neighborhood
stood down in her hips
and preached to me
her words like rolling pins
smoothing out the truth:

> "how you gone get anything done for us
> sitting on the platform for them?"

She had heard about us
Black women
waiting our turn to talk about men
(our fury came out in stereo)
and when we were finished
(our speeches were the longest
we tossed our heads as if our afros
could move in the winds.

There we were,
sitting on the platform
waiting our turn
to talk about men
Black men
how they oppress us
enslave us
abuse us
abandon us
never having wanted us
in the first place.

Black women,
so busy talking on their platforms
we have no time
for Black conferences
Black schools
Black communities
and Black women
who need our bonding
more than white women
need our words

That's what Miss Rosie said
dumping the magnolia blossoms
that had turned brown in her dish.

"You know about this tree?
Don't never change.
Gonna always be magnolia.

Got its own history
its own flowers
its own roots.

Don't never change.
Born magnolia
Gonna stay magnolia.

They like that.
Born a certain way.
Got their own history and roots
and branches and . . . .

Don't never change."

She said something about acorns
and oak trees and faith and Black women
and. . . .

I hope you understand why . . .
I mean . . . ,
You see, Miss Rosie told me. . .

RSVP:
I won't attend the conference
this year
or next year
or ever
until . . .
I
AM
GOING
HOME.

Pretenders

They are people of pretense
playing a game of self-delusion
magicians really
working with trap doors
trick mirrors
puffs of smoke
and marked cards
that tell everything,
and nothing.

They believe in their own illusions
but once off stage
they open locked closets
where skeletons stand erect
clicking the truth.

To White Women Who Come with Words Only

I know you.
I can trace the lines in your hands
without touching you and recite
your history without speaking your name.

I know your fragrance
the length of your hair
the color of your eyes
and the whine of your voice
when you talk passionately
about changing the world.

I have known you since
the beginning when you did not
know me except in your nightmares
which at daybreak you quickly forgot.

I can imitate the way you move your hands
to make a point, an old point,
now dulled from inaction.
I can use Freud and Jung
(who never studied us) to analyze your guilt
which mires you in condescension or sympathy,
neither of which I want or need,
and will not accept

I know you well enough to know
you <u>are</u> sincere about being sincere
about changing the world.
You can do that, you tell me,
and you will, if only I would
tone down my rage
and tear down my wall of distrust

(which, by the way, Black women before me
built brick by brick with their own hands)

I know you
know your needs
know your fears
know even your pain
know from memory your call
for alliances because
after all, you say,
we <u>are</u> women
and women <u>together</u>
can change the world.

Indeed!

But who will fight the enemy
where he lives and sleeps and plays
if you don't

and if you don't
how can <u>we</u> change anything?

When you pull up your carpets
smash your chandaliers
tear up your hymnals
burn your sorority emblems
challenge your men
and bus your children
we can talk

really talk
like sisters
like women
who can
and will
change the world.

For White Women Who Choose Libertion

(a poem for Fannie)

A white woman
with thin lips
cannot sing my songs

with sliding hips
cannot dance my rhythms
with guilt pulsing
through her blue veins
cannot hold my hand
tightly in friendship.

She is the cameo of beauty
lynching my men
pulling the rope
without touching it
from pedestals
I polish to a spitting shine.

A white woman, if wise,
would run from my rage
hide her hair, her skin
her eyes that saw
and often smiled.

You, my friend,
walk toward my rage
meeting it with your own.

You gave us your hand
your heart
your daughters
whose blonde hair

did not stop the charge
of angry men who wore your color
only.

We need no scales
to weigh the pain
the pounds of flesh
the rivers of blood
the screams of women
whose bound hands
cannot stop the violation
cannot rescue loved ones
in slave ships
at auction blocks
on sycamore magnolia   oak
on trains without windows
moving slowly to camps
where there are ovens
fired for death.

Our trust builds
a cauldron in which
we mix the blood
yours
mine
theirs
flowing profusely

in reservations where the mountains weep
in ghettoes where broken people
weary of weeping smile despair
in distant lands where the weeping
is hidden in back pages

that will not print the truth,
but we hear it,
you and I,
riding the waters
cutting the air
moving under the earth like tremors
reaching us
from swamp lands in Nicaguara
rice paddies in Vietnam
public squares in China
desert storms in Kuwait
from hell's hell called South Africa
where my people who weep
for those slain can be slain
for weeping, and are

We drink the blood in silence
light candles in silence
and in the thunderous sound
of change, we call our new name
"Blood sisters."

So go ahead,
my friend,
and hold my hand.

AND THE WOMEN GATHERED

AND THE WOMEN GATHERED.

AND THE WOMEN GATHERED.

AND THE WOMEN GATHERED.

thin women
stout women

short women
tall women

young women
not so young women

flat chested women
big bosomed women

women with blue eyes
green eyes
brown eyes

women with silky hair
curly hair
bleached hair
permed hair

graying hair

AND THE WOMEN GATHERED

coming by planes
busses
vans
cars
trains

and strong feet never tired

TO GATHER

FOR FREEDOM.

married women
divorced women
single women
widowed women

THE WOMEN GATHERED

cocoa
cream
nut brown
beige
caramel
fudge
blackberry black

as diffferent as the stars that grace
the night

THE WOMEN GATHERED

as one constellation.

and the world took notice
that women are warriors

      (always have been,
         even in the beginning)

AND SO THEY GATHERED

AS WOMEN WILL

in the very eye of the storm
pushing against its fury
with their own

and the world took notice
that women birth babies

and REVOLUTIONS.

THE WOMEN GATHERRED

TEN THOUSAND ROSAS INSPIRED
BY ONE.

You saw them.
You saw them.
You saw them.
You saw them.

THE WORLD SAW THEM.

MONTAGE   FROM   THE   MOVEMENT:
HEADLINES

MONTGOMERY, ALABAMA

December 1, 1955 Rosa Parks, a seamstress in Montgomery Alabama, refused to surrender her seat to a white man when ordered by a local bus driver. The Montgomery Bus Boycott begins. Blacks walk, walk, walk for freedom and dignity.

WOMEN WERE THERE.

GREENSBORO, NORTH CAROLINA

February 1, 1960 Students sit in at lunch counters Are refused service. Return. Are arrested. A wave of sit-ins spreads to fifteen cities in five southern states.

WOMEN WERE THERE.

May 4, 1961

The Freedom Rides begin. Blacks and whites ride together on a chartered bus. Savage beatings, arson, legal harrassment.

WOMEN WERE THERE.

BIRMINGHAM

April 3, 1963

Bull Connor turns on waters hoses and unleashes ferocious dogs. Physical violence. Mass arrests. Bombings.

WOMEN WERE THERE.

BIRMINGHAM

September 15, 1963

Four young black girls are killed in church bombing.

MISSISSIPPI, Summer of 1964

Civil Rights activists, Blacks and whites, "invade" the state, registering voters, establishing Freedom Schools . . . .

WOMEN WERE THERE

THE SOUTH

During the course of one year, 80 people were physically assaulted, 30 buildings bombed, 1000 arrested, and 5 murdered.

WOMEN WERE THERE.

SELMA February 1 - March 25

Activists launch a voter registration drive. Hundreds attacked by police wielding "billy clubs," tear gas, whips, and cattle prods as they attempted to march across the Edmund Pettis bridge in Selma.

WOMEN WERE THERE.

Throughout the movement,
Women sang the songs passionately.

>"We shall not. We shall not be moved."

>"Woke up this morning with my mind stayed on freedom."

>"Ain't gonna let-a nobody turn me round, turn me round."

>"Oh Freedom. Oh Freedom.
>Oh Freedom over me.
>And before I'll be a slave,
>I'll be buried in my grave
>and go home to my Lord
>and be free."

AND THE WOMEN GATHERED

in need of empowerment for
themselves
but they gathered
to change the South.

THEY GATHERED
BECAUSE WOMEN DO NOT SLEEP
THROUGH NIGHTMARES.

We shall not call the roll.
It is as long as the Nile
where civilization was born.

We shall not call the roll.
The women wore their courage
and not their names.

It is that way with women.

And so we say

    WOMEN WARRIORS

    TRAILBLAZERS

    TORCHBEARERS

    ACTIVISTS

THINKERS

MOVERS AND SHAKERS

DREAMERS

REVOLUTIONARIES

WE SALUTE YOU.

And we promise
that we will not
sleep through the nightmares

of homelessness, unemployment,
poverty, violence against
children, women, men,
ignorance
oppression of all kinds.

We promise that
a new generation
of WOMEN
will gather.

WE ARE THAT GENERATION.

Feeling Low

I need to write a poem
a deep-down-coming-from-my-guts poem
a healing-like-from-heaven poem
a sweet-song-you-never-heard-before poem

a poem with words
like magic wands
rhythms like heartbeats
colors like rainbows
music other than the blues

which is what I feel
which is why I need this poem
which is why it runs from me

Untitled

Age
writes in spider webs
its bold signature
on legs that have
stood too long
walked too far
and carried too much
through one season after another
season after . . .

The Lesson

from my enemies
i have learned
    to brandish my fist
    at those who would bind my hands
    in helplessness

    to throw my anger
    like a poisoned dart
    at those who have misused me

    to make voodoo dolls
    of those who have strategies
    for my destruction

    to be ice cold in my hate
    and untouchable in my arrogance

and from my friends
whom i have loved
    totally
    fearlessly
    unashamedly
i have learned to carry
    deep and cutting pain
    with quiet dignity.

Platitudes

"The poor shall always be with us."

Tell that to the able-bodied men
who huddle broken at busy street corners
or to women whose children wish for toys
warm beds, and sane parents.

"Ask and it shall be given. Seek and ye shall find."

Tell that to the poor in threadbare clothes
who walk without direction on cold winter streets
carrying their past present and future
in wrinkled paper bags
searching for grates, shelters, soup-
kitchens or kind passers-by who do not fear
their toothless smiles.

"God is merciful, kind and all-loving."

Tell that to the mothers in Africa
who sit in catatonic grief
holding saucer-eyed babies
too weak from starvation
to blink away the flies
that have no knowledge of God.

"We'll understand it better by and by"
in another world.

Tell that to those who
suffer here, and bleed here,

They will not be comforted.

It's All the Same

for all of us

being born

taking deep breaths
gasping
climbing
falling
limping
strutting
loving
hating
crying
shouting
winning
losing
growing old

dying

It's all the same.

Why, then, divisions?

Loss

They tell me I am grieving
that even when I wear pastels
bright enough to pale the sun
I am shrouded in black

that even when I smile
I am damming back tears
that should they fall
would be ten fathoms
deep in sorrow.

They ask me,
"What have you lost?"

and I give different answers
depending on the place
the hour
the color of the sky
or the lingering sounds
of remembered nightmares:

a parent
a child
a love
a song
a dream
a world

where no one loses
the will to make a world
where everyone finds
what is needed desired deserved
or what on dark insane days
might have been lost.

Recovery

Those who waddle in pain
are ignorant of the seasons
which announce recovery
from everything

Those who hold on to darkness
have not seen the sun
curve colors after the rain
and warm the earth.

Unwanted Guest

Do not give hospitality
to misery who sometimes
comes into our lives
when we are on our way
out to happiness

She will play games
with your mind
and suffocate your dreams
in a wide-bosomed embrace
of pity for women only.

Tape your bell.
Double-bolt your door.
Draw your blinds.
Position your most ferocious
watchdog a block from your gate.
Do anything to keep her
out!

If she slips in through a door
you left slightly ajar
in a moment of weakness,
show her the sofa
offer her a cold glass of water
and while she waits for your return
make a quick and secret departure.

When I Was a Child

      I once thought when I was a child
      that being grown was exciting, wild
      like
> happy dancing from winter to spring
> spending money or any ole' thing
> or going where there was lots of fun
> and being always on the run
> and ever carefree.

      I would dream
      I was older
      doing things
      dif'rent and
      bolder
> than catching butterflies by the wing
> and hearing humdrum crickets sing
> or fantasizing I traveled far on backs
> of bees caught in a jar Mama saved for

me.

      I grew up
      and
      now

      I wish for daffodils
      growing graceful on smooth round hills
      where like a child I'll play
      with butterflies and honeybees.
      There
      I will catch the sun at noon

and keep it full from june to june
and route ugly night in a one-way flight
from my sky
down to the cavern
where childish grownfolk
gasp and die.

Talking to Myself

I have decided to be
POSITIVE
about everything.

That's what I'm going to be.
POSITIVE.
I will sing POSITIVE
think POSITIVE
dream POSITIVE
sweat POSITIVE
cry POSITIVE

So what if . . .
someone is in danger,
I mean real danger
and screaming for help
somewhere in this nobody-blessed-America land,
I am going to hear
POSITIVE
you know,
like at least the voice is still there
and obviously very strong.

POSITIVE.

So what if . . .
the children live in
lean-to shacks
that should have been condemned
and probably were,
I am going to think
POSITIVE

you know,
the weeds squeezing through
splintered planks are signs of hope
something is growing in there
so it can't be all bad.

POSITIVE.

So what if . . .
the young men kill themselves
Monday through Saturday
and even on Sunday
with guns and razors
and white powder that makes
no sound and draws no blood,
I won't weep because
we should be concerned
about the population explosion
and besides, maybe, they went
to a better place called heaven.

POSITIVE.

So what if . . .
somebody's nation pushes the button
and we rush madly to shelters stocked
with cans of beans and yams and beets
and corn and water-stuffed hams and rolls
of gauze and tins of band-aid and made-in-Japan
radios that will carry only static . . . .

I will think
POSITIVE.

Like it might not be that bad
because we can end it all
and start again

POSITIVE.

For a Friend Who Considers Suicide

I have no right to ask you to live
when you have already sharpened the blade
and found the strongest pulse.

You have fought the serpents longer than
the best of us, wrestling with their
thrashing tails and speaking sane above
the sound of their rattlers in your head.

When their fangs pierced your skin again
and again, it was your mouth
not mine
that found the marks
and cleansed your veins,
sucking hard
to stay alive.

But that was then,
you tell me,
and this is now.

You have prepared the poison.
It is your life
and your pain
and your right
to end it all

End it
if you must
but in your note
write in a clear hand
that in the other world
you will remember

these things:

the velvet touch of friendship
the sound of laughing children
the sight of men and women
in their winter years smiling spring
and the feel of lovers you have known
who delivered on their promise
to take you to the heavens.

Before you leave,
tell me you will remember
that you were the loving sister
who prepared feasts for others
from a cupboard bare.

Write that note,
my friend.

It is your antidote.

Fighting My Homophobia

(For My Students Who Shared)

What
else
could they expect from me,
a natural woman,
who loves the nights (and days)
when my natural man
holds me naturally
strokes me naturally
getting and giving pleasure
naturally?

My logic was the logic
of the universe.
Beyond challenge.
Unalterable.
In the divine plan.
In the birthing of the species.

Naturally
I rejected them
straight–up
for creating a way
not created to be the way
to love.

I marched with the righteous
who sought them out
(to straighten them out).
I indicted them wholesale
(my gavel was made of steel)
sure in the logic of my logic
they had no defense

until . . .

names and faces
and voices and eyes
journeyed straight to my heart
with memories of the time when
I knew not, and
loved them.

Gave them praisenames
because I
loved them:
eagleminds
chosen ones
children of the Ancestors
young revolutionaries
straight–up sure
about changing the world.

Nothing had changed,
they told me,
except my eyes
clouded by a logic
which rejected truth:

They
compose symphonies
paint murals
write poems
head nations
start revolutions
birth babies
and prepare the dead for homecoming.

Wherever we are, so may they be also:
in the halls of justice,
in the annals of history,
in the pulpits of churches
and
in
heaven.

Their breath, like mine, is in the
wind of the universe
and in the eye of god
there, too, is their image.

Why, then,
can we judge whom
or how they love?

We can
not.
We should
not.
I will
not
ever again.

    I knew not,
    and loved them.

    I love them still.
    Naturally.

Fear

Before the end
I had wanted to spend the night
riding an African drum
across the heavens
beating a steady rhythm of hope
for my people's heartbeat.

I had wanted to be a carpenter building
a gardener planting
an army conquering
a thief trapping the sun
a magician sending pride
like liquid love into their veins
a midwife pulling out the new birth
they did not know they were carrying.

I had planned to do it all
while they slept
and die easy at dawn
while swollen faces
and pressing hands
prayed for a miracle.

The plane races
its mechanical messages of doom
off-beat shirring
mid-air bucking
take my breath away.

I will bite through the clouds
give up my eyes to the splitting winds
and fall shattered to the world
I would have changed for my people.

What a cruel fate
to face the end with strangers
who do not know how you have lived
and how you had planned

to die.

Anointed to Fly

A Poem for Young Sojouners

creme
straight creme mixed with cinnamon
churned like butter creme

and **tan**

coffee tan
smooth cocoa tan
dusty tan
like the wings on a morning dove
in flight tan

and **brown**

brown like the arms of warrior trees
that refused the rope
brown like fertile fields
unfurrowed unploughed
caramel brown
chestnut brown
chocolote brown

and **yellow**

high yellow
lemon yellow
butterscotch yellow
don't-have-to-defend-myself yellow

and **Black**

panther black
midnight black

intense black
singing freedom black
like won't be diluted grey black

black women
our sisters

we know you well.

you are the
daughters of women
who dipped you whole
in the waters of promise.

You have no achilles heels.

for you are the
daughters of women
who detached their wings
repaired them
and passed them on
to you
that you would fly
soar
like eaglewomen black
beyond the reach
of anyone who wants us buried
again

with hands that cupped breasts for you
they cut the cord
unfurled your wings
released you
and in their woman's voice
they are chanting to the winds you ride,
"Not Fragile"
Not Fragile
Not Fragile
Not Fragile"
but "Handle with care"

we know you well

we see you pirouetting like first
picks for an Alvin Ailey suite on blackness
promenading
strutting
strolling
high-stepping
gliding
walking big-city tough
small-town shy
walking in footprints
you can not yet measure
but must claim as heirlooms
from women
who are legends
and legacies
which name you
black women

we know you well

you are black women
preening with pride
palpitating with passion
stretching for knowledge

empowered empowering Black women
Black chosen women
our sisters
anointed to fly

we know you well

you have come
      from ranch-styles
      split-levels
      estates that own the woods
you have come
      from duplexes
      with walls thin enough
      to stereo sounds of sorrow
you have come
      from tenements shot-guns flats projects
      sharecroppers' borrowed rooms
      that were/are oven-warm with love.

we know you well

before your coming
we stroked your tight-skinned young faces
we touched the center of your tears

we stretched your tender muscles into smiles
we danced like African queens to the rhythm of
your joys
we blended the chords of your symphonysong
and we charted the trajectory of your dreams
across the heavens

like meteors knowing their destination
your dreams will light up the darkness
and from their cradles
flowers will bloom

we know you well

black women before us
who were daughters of black women
who were daughters of black women
who were sisters of sisters
black women
African women
the womb of civilization

taught us to breathe in your breath
to stay alive for you
to tighten the drum for you
to open the books for you
to hand the gavel to you
to move the pen for you
to give the world to you

    and your women's hands
    must change it

we know you well

you have come to find the answers
we give only the questions

you have come to begin your planting season
we will place your hands in the soil

you must dig
you must plant
you must till
you must harvest
the fullest yield
of your blackness
your womanness
your genius
and pass it on

to

black women
our sisters
<u>all</u> sisters
all people
everywhere

whom you must
anoint to fly.

Essayist, critic and poet, **Gloria Wade-Gayles** is the author of *No Crystal Stair: Race and Sex in Black Women's Fiction, 1946-76* (Pilgrim Press 1983), which is the first full-length interdisciplinary study of contemporary Black women's fiction. Wade-Gayles' essays have appeared in *The Atlantic Monthly, Liberator, Callaloo* and *Catalyst*; and in several books on Black women's literature and history. Her poetry has appeared in *Essence, The Black Scholar, First World, Black World, Catalyst* and other magazines. She recently completed a play, *Somebody's Calling My Name,* and is currently a Fellow in the DuBois Institute at Harvard University, where she is completing a critical study of the fiction of Alice Walker with support from the Mellon Foundation. She is professor of English and Women's Studies at Spelman College.